# 50 Spring Season Recipes for Home

By: Kelly Johnson

# Table of Contents

- Asparagus and Lemon Risotto
- Strawberry Spinach Salad with Goat Cheese
- Spring Pea Soup with Mint
- Lemon Herb Grilled Chicken
- Radish and Cucumber Salad
- Fresh Strawberry Shortcake
- Asparagus and Prosciutto Tart
- Zucchini and Corn Fritters
- Herbed Salmon with Spring Vegetables
- Lemon Basil Pasta
- Carrot and Ginger Soup
- Pea and Mint Pesto
- Spring Vegetable Stir-Fry
- Rhubarb Compote
- Green Goddess Salad
- Grilled Lamb Chops with Mint Yogurt Sauce
- Lemon Garlic Shrimp Skewers
- Beet and Orange Salad
- Creamy Avocado Pasta
- Spring Herb Quiche
- Grilled Artichokes with Lemon Aioli
- Chilled Cucumber Soup
- Lemon Raspberry Muffins
- Baked Stuffed Portobello Mushrooms
- Thai Spring Rolls with Peanut Sauce
- Fennel and Apple Salad
- Roasted Vegetable Medley
- Herb-Crusted Chicken Breasts
- Strawberry Rhubarb Crisp
- Arugula and Parmesan Salad
- Lemon Blueberry Scones
- Creamy Polenta with Roasted Tomatoes
- Grilled Veggie Wraps
- Poached Eggs with Asparagus
- Spring Onion and Potato Soup
- Watermelon and Feta Salad

- Honey Mustard Glazed Carrots
- Sautéed Shrimp with Lemon and Garlic
- Citrus Roasted Chicken
- Artichoke and Spinach Dip
- Cherry Tomato and Basil Bruschetta
- Sweet Pea and Ricotta Crostini
- Lemon Dill Baked Cod
- Cauliflower Rice Stir-Fry
- Apricot Glazed Chicken
- Radish and Herb Butter Spread
- Minted Pea and Ricotta Salad
- Grilled Peach and Burrata Salad
- Lemon Thyme Chicken Skewers
- Zucchini Noodles with Pesto

**Asparagus and Lemon Risotto**

## Ingredients:

- **1 cup Arborio rice**
- **1 bunch asparagus** (about 1 pound), trimmed and cut into 1-inch pieces
- **1 small onion**, finely chopped
- **2 cloves garlic**, minced
- **1/2 cup dry white wine** (optional, can substitute with more broth)
- **4 cups chicken or vegetable broth**
- **1/2 cup grated Parmesan cheese**
- **2 tablespoons olive oil**
- **1 tablespoon unsalted butter**
- **Zest and juice of 1 lemon**
- **Salt and freshly ground black pepper**, to taste
- **Fresh parsley**, chopped, for garnish (optional)

## Instructions:

1. **Prepare the Broth:**
    - Heat the chicken or vegetable broth in a saucepan over low heat. Keep it warm throughout the cooking process.
2. **Cook the Asparagus:**
    - In a large skillet or saucepan, heat 1 tablespoon of olive oil over medium heat. Add the asparagus and cook until tender but still crisp, about 3-4 minutes. Remove from the skillet and set aside.
3. **Sauté the Aromatics:**
    - In the same skillet or a large pot, add the remaining tablespoon of olive oil. Sauté the chopped onion over medium heat until it becomes translucent, about 3-4 minutes. Add the minced garlic and cook for an additional 1 minute, until fragrant.
4. **Cook the Rice:**
    - Add the Arborio rice to the pot and stir to coat the rice with the oil and onions. Cook for about 2 minutes until the rice is lightly toasted.
5. **Deglaze with Wine:**
    - If using wine, pour it in and cook until the liquid is mostly absorbed.
6. **Add the Broth:**
    - Begin adding the warm broth to the rice, one ladleful at a time. Stir frequently and let the rice absorb the liquid before adding more. Continue this process until the rice is creamy and cooked through, about 18-20 minutes. You may not need all of the broth.
7. **Finish the Risotto:**
    - Once the rice is cooked and creamy, stir in the cooked asparagus. Add the butter, Parmesan cheese, lemon zest, and lemon juice. Stir until the butter and cheese are melted and incorporated. Season with salt and pepper to taste.

8. **Serve:**
    - Garnish with fresh parsley if desired and serve immediately.

Enjoy your Asparagus and Lemon Risotto! It's a bright, creamy dish that's perfect for a light yet satisfying meal.

**Strawberry Spinach Salad with Goat Cheese**

## Ingredients:

- **4 cups fresh baby spinach**
- **1 cup fresh strawberries**, hulled and sliced
- **1/2 cup crumbled goat cheese**
- **1/4 cup sliced almonds** (toasted if preferred)
- **1/4 red onion**, thinly sliced
- **1/4 cup balsamic vinaigrette** (store-bought or homemade)
- **1 tablespoon honey** (optional, for added sweetness)
- **Salt and freshly ground black pepper**, to taste

## Instructions:

1. **Prepare the Ingredients:**
    - Wash and dry the baby spinach and place it in a large salad bowl.
    - Hull and slice the strawberries. If you prefer, you can also halve them for a different presentation.
    - Thinly slice the red onion.
2. **Toast the Almonds (if desired):**
    - In a small dry skillet over medium heat, toast the sliced almonds until they are golden and fragrant, about 3-4 minutes. Stir frequently to avoid burning. Let cool.
3. **Assemble the Salad:**
    - Add the sliced strawberries, crumbled goat cheese, and red onion to the bowl with spinach.
    - Sprinkle the toasted almonds over the top.
4. **Dress the Salad:**
    - Drizzle the balsamic vinaigrette over the salad. If you like a touch more sweetness, you can whisk in a tablespoon of honey into the vinaigrette before dressing the salad.
    - Toss the salad gently to combine all ingredients and ensure the spinach is lightly coated with the dressing.
5. **Season and Serve:**
    - Season with salt and freshly ground black pepper to taste.
    - Serve immediately for the best freshness and flavor.

This Strawberry Spinach Salad with Goat Cheese is perfect for a light lunch or as a side salad for dinner. The combination of flavors and textures—sweet strawberries, creamy goat cheese, crunchy almonds, and fresh spinach—makes it a real treat!

**Spring Pea Soup with Mint**

## Ingredients:

- **4 cups fresh or frozen peas** (if using frozen, thaw them first)
- **1 large onion**, chopped
- **2 cloves garlic**, minced
- **1 medium potato**, peeled and diced
- **4 cups vegetable or chicken broth**
- **1 tablespoon olive oil**
- **1/4 cup fresh mint leaves** (plus extra for garnish)
- **1 tablespoon lemon juice** (optional, for extra brightness)
- **Salt and freshly ground black pepper**, to taste
- **1/2 cup heavy cream** (optional, for a creamy version)

## Instructions:

1. **Prepare the Ingredients:**
   - If using fresh peas, shell them and set aside.
   - Peel and dice the potato, chop the onion, and mince the garlic.
2. **Sauté the Aromatics:**
   - Heat the olive oil in a large pot over medium heat. Add the chopped onion and cook until it becomes translucent, about 5 minutes.
   - Add the minced garlic and cook for an additional 1 minute until fragrant.
3. **Cook the Vegetables:**
   - Add the diced potato to the pot and cook for about 5 minutes, stirring occasionally.
   - Add the peas and cook for another 2-3 minutes.
4. **Add the Broth:**
   - Pour in the vegetable or chicken broth, bring the mixture to a boil, then reduce the heat and let it simmer for about 15-20 minutes, or until the potatoes and peas are tender.
5. **Blend the Soup:**
   - Remove the pot from heat. Using an immersion blender, blend the soup until smooth. Alternatively, you can transfer the soup in batches to a blender to purée it. If you prefer a chunky texture, you can blend just half of the soup.
6. **Add Mint and Season:**
   - Stir in the fresh mint leaves and blend briefly to incorporate the mint flavor. If you're adding heavy cream, stir it in now and heat the soup gently to warm it through.
   - Season with salt and freshly ground black pepper to taste. If you like a bit more brightness, stir in the lemon juice.
7. **Serve:**
   - Ladle the soup into bowls and garnish with a few fresh mint leaves.

- Serve warm.

This Spring Pea Soup with Mint is light yet flavorful, perfect for a spring or summer meal. The mint adds a refreshing touch that complements the sweetness of the peas beautifully. Enjoy!

**Lemon Herb Grilled Chicken**

## Ingredients:

- 4 boneless, skinless chicken breasts
- 1/4 cup olive oil
- Juice of 1 large lemon
- 2 tablespoons lemon zest
- **3 cloves garlic**, minced
- **1 tablespoon fresh thyme** (or 1 teaspoon dried thyme)
- **1 tablespoon fresh rosemary** (or 1 teaspoon dried rosemary)
- **1 teaspoon dried oregano**
- **Salt and freshly ground black pepper**, to taste

## Instructions:

1. **Prepare the Marinade:**
   - In a bowl, whisk together the olive oil, lemon juice, lemon zest, minced garlic, thyme, rosemary, oregano, salt, and black pepper.
2. **Marinate the Chicken:**
   - Place the chicken breasts in a large resealable plastic bag or shallow dish. Pour the marinade over the chicken, ensuring all pieces are well coated.
   - Seal the bag or cover the dish and refrigerate for at least 30 minutes, or up to 2 hours for more flavor. If you're short on time, even 15 minutes can add some great flavor.
3. **Preheat the Grill:**
   - Preheat your grill to medium-high heat. Clean and oil the grill grates to prevent sticking.
4. **Grill the Chicken:**
   - Remove the chicken from the marinade and let any excess drip off. Place the chicken on the grill.
   - Grill the chicken for about 6-8 minutes per side, or until the internal temperature reaches 165°F (74°C) and the juices run clear. The exact time will depend on the thickness of the chicken breasts.
5. **Rest and Serve:**
   - Once cooked, remove the chicken from the grill and let it rest for 5 minutes before slicing. This helps retain the juices.
   - Garnish with extra lemon slices or fresh herbs if desired.

## Tips:

- **Even Cooking:** For more even cooking, consider pounding the chicken breasts to an even thickness before marinating and grilling.

- **Grill Marks:** To get nice grill marks, avoid moving the chicken around too much while grilling.

This Lemon Herb Grilled Chicken is perfect for a light summer meal and goes well with a variety of sides like roasted vegetables, salads, or a fresh quinoa dish. Enjoy!

**Radish and Cucumber Salad**

## Ingredients:

- **1 bunch radishes**, thinly sliced (about 10-12 radishes)
- **1 large cucumber**, peeled and sliced (or leave the skin on for extra crunch)
- **1/4 red onion**, thinly sliced (optional)
- **2 tablespoons fresh dill** (or 1 tablespoon dried dill)
- **2 tablespoons fresh parsley**, chopped
- **1 tablespoon olive oil**
- **1 tablespoon white wine vinegar** (or apple cider vinegar)
- **1 teaspoon lemon juice**
- **1/2 teaspoon sugar** (optional, to balance the flavors)
- **Salt and freshly ground black pepper**, to taste

## Instructions:

1. **Prepare the Vegetables:**
   - Thinly slice the radishes and cucumber. If you're using a cucumber with a tough skin, peel it before slicing. You can also cut the cucumber into half-moons or rounds based on your preference.
   - If using, thinly slice the red onion.
2. **Make the Dressing:**
   - In a small bowl, whisk together the olive oil, white wine vinegar, lemon juice, and sugar (if using). Season with salt and freshly ground black pepper to taste.
3. **Assemble the Salad:**
   - In a large bowl, combine the sliced radishes, cucumber, and red onion (if using). Toss to mix.
   - Pour the dressing over the vegetables and toss gently to coat.
4. **Add Fresh Herbs:**
   - Stir in the fresh dill and parsley.
5. **Chill and Serve:**
   - Let the salad sit for about 10-15 minutes before serving to allow the flavors to meld. You can also refrigerate it for a cooler, refreshing option.
6. **Adjust Seasoning:**
   - Taste and adjust seasoning with more salt, pepper, or a bit more vinegar if needed.

This Radish and Cucumber Salad is crisp, light, and has a great mix of flavors that make it a perfect side dish for grilled meats, sandwiches, or as part of a larger spread. Enjoy!

**Fresh Strawberry Shortcake**

## Ingredients:

**For the Strawberries:**

- **1 pound fresh strawberries**, hulled and sliced
- **1/4 cup granulated sugar**

**For the Shortcakes:**

- **2 cups all-purpose flour**
- **1/4 cup granulated sugar**
- **1 tablespoon baking powder**
- **1/2 teaspoon salt**
- **1/2 cup cold unsalted butter**, cut into small cubes
- **3/4 cup whole milk**
- **1 large egg**
- **1 teaspoon vanilla extract**

**For the Whipped Cream:**

- **1 cup heavy cream**
- **2 tablespoons powdered sugar**
- **1 teaspoon vanilla extract**

## Instructions:

1. **Prepare the Strawberries:**
    - In a medium bowl, toss the sliced strawberries with the granulated sugar. Let them sit for about 30 minutes to an hour, allowing the sugar to draw out the juices and create a syrup.
2. **Make the Shortcakes:**
    - Preheat your oven to 425°F (220°C). Line a baking sheet with parchment paper.
    - In a large bowl, whisk together the flour, sugar, baking powder, and salt.
    - Add the cold butter cubes to the flour mixture. Using a pastry cutter or your fingers, cut the butter into the flour until the mixture resembles coarse crumbs.
    - In a separate bowl, whisk together the milk, egg, and vanilla extract.
    - Pour the wet ingredients into the dry ingredients and stir until just combined. The dough will be slightly sticky.
    - Turn the dough onto a floured surface and gently knead it a few times until it comes together. Pat the dough into a 1-inch thick rectangle. Use a round cutter (about 2 1/2 inches in diameter) to cut out the shortcakes. Re-roll and cut out any remaining dough.

- Place the shortcakes on the prepared baking sheet and bake for 12-15 minutes, or until golden brown. Allow to cool slightly before serving.
3. **Prepare the Whipped Cream:**
    - In a mixing bowl, combine the heavy cream, powdered sugar, and vanilla extract.
    - Using an electric mixer, beat the cream on high speed until soft peaks form.
4. **Assemble the Shortcakes:**
    - Split the shortcakes in half horizontally. Spoon a generous amount of the sugared strawberries and their juice over the bottom half of each shortcake.
    - Top with a dollop of whipped cream.
    - Place the top half of the shortcake over the whipped cream and garnish with additional strawberries and whipped cream if desired.

## Tips:

- **For Extra Flavor:** Add a splash of vanilla or a pinch of lemon zest to the strawberries for extra flavor.
- **Serving Suggestion:** Serve the shortcakes immediately for the best texture, as the biscuits can become soggy if left too long with the strawberries.

Enjoy your Fresh Strawberry Shortcake—a perfect, light dessert to celebrate the strawberry season!

**Asparagus and Prosciutto Tart**

## Ingredients:

**For the Tart Crust:**

- **1 1/4 cups all-purpose flour**
- **1/4 teaspoon salt**
- **1/2 cup cold unsalted butter**, cut into small cubes
- **1/4 cup ice water** (more if needed)

**For the Filling:**

- **1 tablespoon olive oil**
- **1 bunch asparagus** (about 1/2 pound), trimmed and cut into 2-inch pieces
- **4 ounces prosciutto**, sliced
- **1 cup shredded Gruyère cheese** (or Swiss cheese)
- **1/2 cup crème fraîche** (or sour cream)
- **2 large eggs**
- **Salt and freshly ground black pepper**, to taste
- **1 tablespoon fresh thyme leaves** (or 1 teaspoon dried thyme)

## Instructions:

1. **Prepare the Tart Crust:**
    - Preheat your oven to 375°F (190°C).
    - In a food processor, combine the flour and salt. Add the cold butter and pulse until the mixture resembles coarse crumbs.
    - Gradually add the ice water, one tablespoon at a time, until the dough begins to come together. Be careful not to overwork the dough.
    - Transfer the dough to a lightly floured surface and gently knead it into a disk. Roll out the dough to fit a 9-inch tart pan or pie dish.
    - Press the dough into the pan and trim the edges. Prick the bottom of the crust with a fork to prevent bubbling.
    - Bake the crust for about 10 minutes, or until it starts to turn golden. Remove from the oven and let cool slightly.
2. **Prepare the Asparagus:**
    - While the crust is baking, heat the olive oil in a skillet over medium heat. Add the asparagus pieces and cook for about 3-4 minutes, until just tender but still crisp. Season with a little salt and pepper. Remove from heat and set aside.
3. **Assemble the Tart:**
    - In a mixing bowl, whisk together the crème fraîche, eggs, and a pinch of salt and pepper until smooth. Stir in the shredded Gruyère cheese and thyme leaves.
    - Spread the cooked asparagus evenly over the pre-baked tart crust.
    - Tear the prosciutto into pieces and scatter it over the asparagus.

- Pour the crème fraîche mixture over the asparagus and prosciutto, spreading it evenly.
4. **Bake the Tart:**
    - Bake the tart in the preheated oven for 25-30 minutes, or until the filling is set and the top is golden brown.
5. **Serve:**
    - Allow the tart to cool slightly before slicing. Serve warm or at room temperature.

## Tips:

- **For a Flakier Crust:** Use cold butter and keep the dough chilled before baking.
- **Vegetable Variations:** You can substitute or add other vegetables, like mushrooms or cherry tomatoes, if desired.
- **Make Ahead:** The tart can be prepared ahead of time and reheated gently before serving.

Enjoy this Asparagus and Prosciutto Tart as a sophisticated and flavorful dish that's sure to impress!

**Zucchini and Corn Fritters**

## Ingredients:

- **2 medium zucchinis**, grated
- **1 cup corn kernels** (fresh, frozen, or canned)
- **1/2 cup all-purpose flour**
- **1/4 cup cornmeal**
- **2 large eggs**
- **1/4 cup grated Parmesan cheese** (optional, for extra flavor)
- **2 green onions**, chopped
- **1 tablespoon fresh parsley**, chopped (or 1 teaspoon dried parsley)
- **1 teaspoon baking powder**
- **Salt and freshly ground black pepper**, to taste
- **Olive oil** (for frying)

## Instructions:

1. **Prepare the Zucchini:**
    - Place the grated zucchini in a clean cloth or paper towel and squeeze out excess moisture.
2. **Mix the Batter:**
    - In a large bowl, combine the zucchini, corn, flour, cornmeal, eggs, Parmesan cheese (if using), green onions, parsley, baking powder, salt, and pepper. Mix until well combined.
3. **Heat the Oil:**
    - Heat a few tablespoons of olive oil in a large skillet over medium heat.
4. **Fry the Fritters:**
    - Drop spoonfuls of the batter into the hot skillet, flattening them slightly with the back of the spoon. Cook for about 2-3 minutes per side, or until golden brown and crispy.
    - Remove the fritters from the skillet and place them on a paper towel-lined plate to drain any excess oil.
5. **Serve:**
    - Serve the fritters warm with a dollop of sour cream, yogurt, or your favorite dipping sauce.

## Tips:

- **For Extra Crispiness:** Make sure the skillet is hot and the oil is well-heated before adding the fritters.
- **Vegetable Add-Ins:** Feel free to add other vegetables or herbs to the batter for variation.

Enjoy these Zucchini and Corn Fritters as a delightful, crunchy treat!

**Herbed Salmon with Spring Vegetables**

## Ingredients:

- **4 salmon fillets** (6 oz each)
- **1 tablespoon olive oil**
- **1 lemon**, sliced
- **2 tablespoons fresh dill** (or 1 tablespoon dried dill)
- **2 tablespoons fresh parsley**, chopped
- **2 cloves garlic**, minced
- **1 teaspoon dried oregano**
- **Salt and freshly ground black pepper**, to taste

**For the Vegetables:**

- **1 cup baby carrots**
- **1 cup snap peas**
- **1 cup baby potatoes**, halved
- **1 tablespoon olive oil**
- **1 teaspoon dried thyme**
- **Salt and freshly ground black pepper**, to taste

## Instructions:

1. **Preheat Oven:**
   - Preheat your oven to 400°F (200°C).
2. **Prepare the Vegetables:**
   - Toss the baby carrots, snap peas, and baby potatoes with olive oil, dried thyme, salt, and pepper. Spread them on a baking sheet in a single layer.
3. **Prepare the Salmon:**
   - In a small bowl, mix the olive oil, garlic, dill, parsley, oregano, salt, and pepper.
   - Place the salmon fillets on a separate baking sheet lined with parchment paper or lightly greased.
   - Brush the salmon fillets with the herb mixture and top each with a few lemon slices.
4. **Roast the Vegetables:**
   - Roast the vegetables in the preheated oven for 20 minutes, stirring halfway through.
5. **Add the Salmon:**
   - After 20 minutes, add the salmon to the oven with the vegetables. Continue roasting for an additional 12-15 minutes, or until the salmon flakes easily with a fork and the vegetables are tender.
6. **Serve:**
   - Serve the salmon fillets with the roasted spring vegetables.

## Tips:

- **For Crispy Skin:** Place the salmon skin-side down and avoid moving it around while cooking.
- **Vegetable Variations:** Feel free to add other spring vegetables like asparagus or radishes if desired.

Enjoy your Herbed Salmon with Spring Vegetables—a wholesome and satisfying dish that's perfect for a fresh, seasonal meal!

**Lemon Basil Pasta**

## Ingredients:

- **8 oz (225g) pasta** (such as spaghetti, linguine, or fettuccine)
- **2 tablespoons olive oil**
- **2 cloves garlic**, minced
- **1 lemon**, zested and juiced
- **1/2 cup grated Parmesan cheese**
- **1/4 cup fresh basil leaves**, chopped (plus extra for garnish)
- **Salt and freshly ground black pepper**, to taste
- **Red pepper flakes** (optional, for a touch of heat)

## Instructions:

1. **Cook the Pasta:**
   - Cook the pasta according to the package instructions until al dente. Reserve 1/2 cup of pasta cooking water, then drain the pasta.
2. **Prepare the Sauce:**
   - In a large skillet, heat the olive oil over medium heat. Add the minced garlic and sauté for about 1 minute, until fragrant but not browned.
3. **Combine Pasta and Sauce:**
   - Add the cooked pasta to the skillet with the garlic. Toss to coat the pasta with the garlic oil.
   - Stir in the lemon zest and juice, and add a splash of the reserved pasta cooking water if needed to help loosen the sauce and coat the pasta evenly.
4. **Add Cheese and Basil:**
   - Remove the skillet from heat. Stir in the grated Parmesan cheese and chopped basil. Toss until the cheese is melted and the basil is evenly distributed. Season with salt, pepper, and red pepper flakes (if using) to taste.
5. **Serve:**
   - Divide the pasta among serving plates. Garnish with additional fresh basil and a bit more Parmesan cheese if desired.

## Tips:

- **Pasta Cooking Water:** Adding a bit of reserved pasta cooking water helps to create a silkier sauce.
- **Variations:** You can add vegetables like cherry tomatoes, spinach, or peas for extra flavor and nutrition.
- **Protein Additions:** For added protein, consider topping the pasta with grilled chicken, shrimp, or a poached egg.

This Lemon Basil Pasta is bright and refreshing, making it a perfect choice for a light lunch or a quick weeknight dinner. Enjoy!

**Carrot and Ginger Soup**

**Ingredients:**

- **1 tablespoon olive oil**
- **1 medium onion**, chopped
- **2 cloves garlic**, minced
- **1 tablespoon fresh ginger**, grated (or 1 teaspoon ground ginger)
- **1 pound carrots**, peeled and chopped
- **4 cups vegetable or chicken broth**
- **1/2 teaspoon ground cumin** (optional, for extra warmth)
- **Salt and freshly ground black pepper**, to taste
- **1/4 cup heavy cream** (optional, for a creamy finish)
- **Fresh parsley or cilantro**, chopped, for garnish (optional)

## Instructions:

1. **Sauté Aromatics:**
    - Heat the olive oil in a large pot over medium heat. Add the chopped onion and cook until translucent, about 5 minutes.
    - Add the minced garlic and grated ginger, and cook for another 1-2 minutes, until fragrant.
2. **Cook the Carrots:**
    - Add the chopped carrots to the pot and cook for about 5 minutes, stirring occasionally.
3. **Add Broth and Spices:**
    - Pour in the vegetable or chicken broth and add the ground cumin (if using). Bring the mixture to a boil, then reduce the heat and simmer until the carrots are tender, about 20 minutes.
4. **Blend the Soup:**
    - Remove the pot from heat. Using an immersion blender, blend the soup until smooth. Alternatively, you can carefully transfer the soup in batches to a blender. Be sure to let the soup cool slightly before blending to avoid splatters.
5. **Finish and Season:**
    - Return the soup to the pot (if using a blender). Stir in the heavy cream, if desired, and heat through.
    - Season with salt and pepper to taste.
6. **Serve:**
    - Ladle the soup into bowls and garnish with fresh parsley or cilantro if desired.

## Tips:

- **For Extra Flavor:** Add a pinch of ground coriander or a splash of orange juice for additional depth of flavor.
- **Make Ahead:** This soup can be made ahead of time and stored in the refrigerator for up to 4 days. It also freezes well for up to 3 months.

Enjoy your Carrot and Ginger Soup—it's a delightful, warming dish that's perfect for cozying up on a cool day!

**Pea and Mint Pesto**

**Ingredients:**

- **1 cup frozen peas** (thawed) or fresh peas
- **1/2 cup fresh mint leaves**
- **1/4 cup fresh basil leaves** (optional, for added flavor)
- **1/4 cup pine nuts** (or almonds or walnuts)
- **1/4 cup grated Parmesan cheese**
- **1/4 cup olive oil**
- **1-2 cloves garlic**, minced
- **Juice of 1 lemon**
- **Salt and freshly ground black pepper**, to taste

## Instructions:

1. **Prepare the Ingredients:**
   - If using frozen peas, thaw them by placing them in a bowl of warm water for a few minutes, then drain. If using fresh peas, blanch them briefly in boiling water for 1-2 minutes and then cool in ice water.
2. **Blend the Pesto:**
   - In a food processor, combine the peas, mint leaves, basil (if using), pine nuts, Parmesan cheese, garlic, and lemon juice. Pulse until the mixture is finely chopped.
3. **Add Olive Oil:**
   - With the food processor running, slowly stream in the olive oil until the pesto reaches your desired consistency. You may need to scrape down the sides of the bowl occasionally.
4. **Season and Adjust:**
   - Season with salt and pepper to taste. Adjust the consistency with more olive oil if needed, and add more lemon juice for extra brightness if desired.
5. **Serve:**
   - Use the pesto immediately or store it in an airtight container in the refrigerator for up to 1 week. You can also freeze it for up to 3 months.

## Tips:

- **For Creaminess:** Add a little more Parmesan cheese or a splash of cream for a richer texture.
- **Variations:** Feel free to experiment with other nuts or herbs based on your preference.

Enjoy your Pea and Mint Pesto as a fresh and flavorful addition to your dishes!

**Spring Vegetable Stir-Fry**

## Ingredients:

- **2 tablespoons vegetable oil**
- **1 cup snap peas**
- **1 cup asparagus**, cut into 2-inch pieces
- **1 cup baby carrots**, sliced
- **1 red bell pepper**, sliced
- **1 cup mushrooms**, sliced
- **2 cloves garlic**, minced
- **1 tablespoon fresh ginger**, minced
- **3 green onions**, sliced
- **1/4 cup soy sauce** (or tamari for gluten-free)
- **1 tablespoon hoisin sauce** (optional)
- **1 tablespoon sesame oil**
- **1 teaspoon cornstarch** mixed with 1 tablespoon water (for thickening, optional)
- **Sesame seeds** and **fresh cilantro**, for garnish (optional)
- **Cooked rice** or **noodles**, for serving

## Instructions:

1. **Prepare the Ingredients:**
   - Wash and cut the vegetables as needed. Mix the cornstarch with water in a small bowl to make a slurry if using.
2. **Heat the Oil:**
   - Heat the vegetable oil in a large skillet or wok over medium-high heat.
3. **Cook the Vegetables:**
   - Add the garlic and ginger to the skillet and sauté for 1 minute until fragrant.
   - Add the snap peas, asparagus, baby carrots, and mushrooms. Stir-fry for 3-4 minutes until the vegetables are tender-crisp.
4. **Add Bell Pepper and Sauce:**
   - Add the red bell pepper and cook for an additional 2 minutes.
   - Stir in the soy sauce, hoisin sauce (if using), and sesame oil. Cook for 1-2 minutes until everything is well-coated and heated through.
5. **Thicken Sauce (Optional):**
   - If you prefer a thicker sauce, add the cornstarch slurry to the pan and stir well. Cook for an additional 1-2 minutes until the sauce thickens.
6. **Garnish and Serve:**
   - Remove from heat and garnish with sesame seeds and fresh cilantro if desired.
   - Serve the stir-fry over cooked rice or noodles.

## Tips:

- **Customize:** Feel free to add or substitute other seasonal vegetables like baby corn, zucchini, or bell peppers.
- **Protein:** For added protein, you can include tofu, chicken, or shrimp.

Enjoy your vibrant and nutritious Spring Vegetable Stir-Fry!

**Rhubarb Compote**

**Ingredients:**

- **4 cups rhubarb**, chopped into 1/2-inch pieces
- **1 cup granulated sugar** (adjust based on the tartness of your rhubarb)
- **1/2 cup water**
- **1 teaspoon vanilla extract**
- **1 tablespoon lemon juice**
- **1/4 teaspoon ground ginger** (optional, for extra warmth)
- **1/4 teaspoon ground cinnamon** (optional, for added depth)

## Instructions:

1. **Prepare the Rhubarb:**
   - Wash and chop the rhubarb into 1/2-inch pieces. Discard any leaves, as they are toxic.
2. **Cook the Compote:**
   - In a medium saucepan, combine the chopped rhubarb, granulated sugar, and water.
   - Bring to a boil over medium-high heat, stirring occasionally.
3. **Simmer:**
   - Reduce the heat to low and simmer for about 10-15 minutes, or until the rhubarb has broken down and the mixture has thickened to a sauce-like consistency. Stir occasionally to prevent sticking.
4. **Add Flavorings:**
   - Stir in the vanilla extract, lemon juice, and optional spices (ground ginger and cinnamon) if using. Cook for an additional 1-2 minutes.
5. **Cool and Store:**
   - Remove from heat and let the compote cool to room temperature. It will thicken further as it cools.
   - Transfer to a jar or airtight container and refrigerate. The compote can be stored in the refrigerator for up to 2 weeks.

## Tips:

- **Adjust Sweetness:** Taste the compote before adding the vanilla and spices. If it's too tart, you can add more sugar to balance the flavor.
- **Texture:** If you prefer a smoother texture, you can use an immersion blender to puree the compote slightly.

Enjoy your Rhubarb Compote as a delightful addition to various dishes or simply on its own!

**Green Goddess Salad**

## Ingredients:

**For the Salad:**

- **4 cups mixed greens** (such as romaine, spinach, arugula, or kale)
- **1 cup cucumber**, sliced
- **1 cup cherry tomatoes**, halved
- **1/2 cup radishes**, thinly sliced
- **1 avocado**, diced
- **1/4 cup red onion**, thinly sliced
- **1/4 cup fresh parsley**, chopped
- **1/4 cup fresh basil**, chopped
- **1/4 cup fresh chives**, chopped (optional)

**For the Green Goddess Dressing:**

- **1 cup fresh basil leaves**
- **1/2 cup fresh parsley leaves**
- **1/4 cup fresh chives** (optional)
- **1/2 cup Greek yogurt** (or sour cream)
- **2 tablespoons lemon juice**
- **2 cloves garlic**, minced
- **2 tablespoons olive oil**
- **Salt and freshly ground black pepper**, to taste

## Instructions:

1. **Prepare the Dressing:**
    - In a food processor or blender, combine the basil, parsley, chives (if using), Greek yogurt, lemon juice, garlic, and olive oil. Blend until smooth.
    - Season with salt and pepper to taste. Adjust the consistency with a little water if needed to reach your desired thickness.
2. **Prepare the Salad:**
    - In a large salad bowl, combine the mixed greens, cucumber, cherry tomatoes, radishes, avocado, red onion, and fresh herbs (parsley, basil, chives).
    - Toss gently to mix the vegetables.
3. **Dress the Salad:**
    - Drizzle the Green Goddess Dressing over the salad and toss gently to coat all the ingredients evenly.
4. **Serve:**
    - Serve immediately, or chill the salad and dressing separately until ready to serve. Toss the salad with the dressing just before serving to keep the greens crisp.

## Tips:

- **For Extra Protein:** Add grilled chicken, tofu, or chickpeas to make the salad a complete meal.

- **Variations:** Feel free to add other vegetables like bell peppers, celery, or olives based on your preference.

This Green Goddess Salad is both nutritious and delicious, with a refreshing dressing that brings out the best in your fresh vegetables. Enjoy!

**Grilled Lamb Chops with Mint Yogurt Sauce**

**Ingredients:**

**For the Lamb Chops:**

- **8 lamb chops** (about 1-inch thick)
- **2 tablespoons olive oil**
- **2 cloves garlic**, minced
- **1 tablespoon fresh rosemary** (or 1 teaspoon dried rosemary), chopped
- **1 tablespoon fresh thyme** (or 1 teaspoon dried thyme), chopped
- **Salt and freshly ground black pepper**, to taste

**For the Mint Yogurt Sauce:**

- **1 cup Greek yogurt**
- **1/2 cup fresh mint leaves**, chopped
- **1 tablespoon lemon juice**
- **1 tablespoon olive oil**
- **1 clove garlic**, minced
- **Salt and freshly ground black pepper**, to taste

## Instructions:

1. **Marinate the Lamb Chops:**
    - In a small bowl, mix the olive oil, minced garlic, rosemary, thyme, salt, and pepper.
    - Rub the mixture over the lamb chops, coating them evenly. Let them marinate for at least 30 minutes (or up to 2 hours) in the refrigerator.
2. **Prepare the Mint Yogurt Sauce:**
    - In a bowl, combine the Greek yogurt, chopped mint, lemon juice, olive oil, minced garlic, salt, and pepper.
    - Mix well and refrigerate until ready to serve.
3. **Grill the Lamb Chops:**
    - Preheat your grill to medium-high heat.
    - Grill the lamb chops for about 4-5 minutes per side for medium-rare, or longer if desired. Use a meat thermometer to check for doneness (130°F/54°C for medium-rare).
4. **Serve:**
    - Remove the lamb chops from the grill and let them rest for a few minutes.
    - Serve with the chilled mint yogurt sauce on the side.

## Tips:

- **For Extra Flavor:** Add a squeeze of lemon juice over the lamb chops just before serving.
- **Side Suggestions:** Pair the lamb chops with roasted vegetables or a fresh salad.

Enjoy your Grilled Lamb Chops with Mint Yogurt Sauce—a delicious and sophisticated dish that's sure to impress!

**Lemon Garlic Shrimp Skewers**

**Ingredients:**

- **1 pound large shrimp**, peeled and deveined
- **3 tablespoons olive oil**
- **3 cloves garlic**, minced
- **Zest and juice of 1 lemon**
- **1 teaspoon dried oregano** (or 1 tablespoon fresh oregano)
- **1/2 teaspoon paprika**
- **Salt and freshly ground black pepper**, to taste
- **Wooden or metal skewers**

## Instructions:

1. **Prepare the Marinade:**
   - In a bowl, combine the olive oil, minced garlic, lemon zest, lemon juice, dried oregano, paprika, salt, and pepper.
2. **Marinate the Shrimp:**
   - Add the shrimp to the marinade, tossing to coat them evenly. Let the shrimp marinate for at least 15 minutes (or up to 1 hour) in the refrigerator.
3. **Prepare the Skewers:**
   - If using wooden skewers, soak them in water for at least 30 minutes to prevent burning.
   - Thread the marinated shrimp onto the skewers.
4. **Grill the Shrimp:**
   - Preheat your grill to medium-high heat.
   - Grill the shrimp skewers for 2-3 minutes per side, or until the shrimp are opaque and cooked through.
5. **Serve:**
   - Remove the shrimp from the grill and serve immediately. They pair well with a fresh salad, rice, or grilled vegetables.

## Tips:

- **For Added Flavor:** Brush the shrimp with a little more marinade or olive oil while grilling for extra moisture.
- **Side Options:** Consider serving with a lemon wedge or a side of tzatziki sauce for a refreshing complement.

Enjoy your Lemon Garlic Shrimp Skewers—perfect for a quick and tasty meal!

**Beet and Orange Salad**

## Ingredients:

- **4 medium beets**, roasted or boiled
- **2 large oranges**, peeled and segmented
- **1/4 cup red onion**, thinly sliced
- **1/4 cup crumbled feta cheese** (optional)
- **2 tablespoons fresh parsley**, chopped
- **1 tablespoon fresh mint**, chopped (optional)
- **1/4 cup walnuts** or **pecans**, toasted (optional)
- **2 tablespoons olive oil**
- **1 tablespoon balsamic vinegar** or **red wine vinegar**
- **1 teaspoon honey** or **maple syrup**
- **Salt and freshly ground black pepper**, to taste

## Instructions:

1. **Prepare the Beets:**
   - **To Roast:** Preheat your oven to 400°F (200°C). Wrap each beet in aluminum foil and place them on a baking sheet. Roast for 45-60 minutes, or until tender when pierced with a fork. Let cool, then peel and slice.
   - **To Boil:** Place the beets in a pot of boiling water and cook for 30-40 minutes until tender. Let cool, then peel and slice.
2. **Prepare the Salad Components:**
   - Peel and segment the oranges over a bowl to catch any juice. Remove any seeds and set the segments aside.
   - Thinly slice the red onion.
   - Toast the walnuts or pecans in a dry skillet over medium heat until fragrant, about 3-4 minutes.
3. **Make the Dressing:**
   - In a small bowl, whisk together the olive oil, balsamic vinegar (or red wine vinegar), honey (or maple syrup), salt, and pepper until well combined.
4. **Assemble the Salad:**
   - Arrange the beet slices on a serving platter or individual plates.
   - Scatter the orange segments, red onion slices, and crumbled feta cheese (if using) over the beets.
   - Drizzle with the dressing and sprinkle with chopped parsley, mint (if using), and toasted nuts.
5. **Serve:**
   - Serve the salad immediately or refrigerate it for up to an hour before serving. It can be enjoyed cold or at room temperature.

## Tips:

- **For Added Texture:** Use a mix of red and golden beets for more color contrast.
- **Make Ahead:** You can roast or boil the beets in advance to save time. The salad is best assembled just before serving to keep the ingredients fresh and vibrant.

Enjoy your Beet and Orange Salad—a delicious and visually stunning dish that's perfect for any occasion!

**Creamy Avocado Pasta**

**Ingredients:**

- **12 oz (340g) pasta** (such as spaghetti, fettuccine, or penne)
- **2 ripe avocados**
- **1/4 cup fresh basil leaves** (or 1 tablespoon dried basil)
- **2 cloves garlic**
- **2 tablespoons lemon juice**
- **1/4 cup olive oil**
- **1/4 cup grated Parmesan cheese** (optional)
- **Salt and freshly ground black pepper**, to taste
- **1/4 cup pine nuts** (optional, for garnish)
- **Cherry tomatoes**, halved (optional, for garnish)

## Instructions:

1. **Cook the Pasta:**
   - Cook the pasta according to the package instructions until al dente. Reserve 1/2 cup of pasta cooking water, then drain the pasta.
2. **Prepare the Avocado Sauce:**
   - In a food processor or blender, combine the avocados, basil leaves, garlic, lemon juice, and olive oil. Blend until smooth and creamy. If the sauce is too thick, add a bit of the reserved pasta cooking water to reach your desired consistency.
3. **Add Cheese (Optional):**
   - Stir in the grated Parmesan cheese if using. Blend again to combine.
4. **Combine Pasta and Sauce:**
   - In a large bowl or pot, toss the cooked pasta with the creamy avocado sauce until well coated. If the sauce is too thick, add more reserved pasta cooking water as needed.
5. **Season and Serve:**
   - Season with salt and freshly ground black pepper to taste.
   - Garnish with toasted pine nuts and halved cherry tomatoes if desired.
6. **Serve Immediately:**
   - Serve the pasta immediately for the best texture.

## Tips:

- **For Extra Flavor:** Add a pinch of red pepper flakes or a bit of chopped sun-dried tomatoes to the sauce for an extra kick.
- **Make It a Meal:** Add grilled chicken, shrimp, or roasted vegetables to the pasta for a complete meal.

Enjoy your Creamy Avocado Pasta—it's a delightful, creamy dish that's both satisfying and healthy!

**Spring Herb Quiche**

**Ingredients:**

**For the Crust:**

- **1 1/2 cups all-purpose flour**
- **1/2 cup cold unsalted butter**, cut into small pieces
- **1/4 cup cold water**
- **1/4 teaspoon salt**

**For the Filling:**

- **1 tablespoon olive oil**
- **1/2 cup onion**, finely chopped
- **1 cup asparagus**, cut into 1-inch pieces
- **1 cup fresh spinach**, chopped
- **1/2 cup fresh parsley**, chopped
- **1/4 cup fresh chives**, chopped
- **4 large eggs**
- **1 cup whole milk**
- **1/2 cup heavy cream**
- **1 cup shredded cheese** (such as Gruyère, cheddar, or feta)
- **Salt and freshly ground black pepper**, to taste

## Instructions:

1. **Prepare the Crust:**
    - In a food processor, pulse the flour and salt. Add the cold butter and pulse until the mixture resembles coarse crumbs.
    - Gradually add the cold water, pulsing until the dough begins to come together.
    - Turn the dough out onto a floured surface, form into a disk, wrap in plastic wrap, and refrigerate for at least 30 minutes.
2. **Preheat Oven:**
    - Preheat your oven to 375°F (190°C).
3. **Roll Out and Pre-Bake the Crust:**
    - On a floured surface, roll out the dough to fit a 9-inch pie or quiche pan. Press the dough into the pan and trim any excess.
    - Line the crust with parchment paper and fill with pie weights or dried beans. Bake for 10 minutes, then remove the weights and parchment. Bake for an additional 5 minutes until lightly golden.
4. **Prepare the Filling:**
    - Heat olive oil in a skillet over medium heat. Add the chopped onion and cook until translucent, about 5 minutes.
    - Add the asparagus and cook for another 3-4 minutes until tender. Stir in the spinach and cook until wilted. Remove from heat and let cool slightly.
5. **Mix the Custard:**
    - In a bowl, whisk together the eggs, milk, and heavy cream. Stir in the cheese, parsley, chives, and the cooked vegetable mixture. Season with salt and pepper.
6. **Assemble and Bake:**

- Pour the filling into the pre-baked crust. Bake in the preheated oven for 35-40 minutes, or until the quiche is set and lightly golden on top.
7. **Cool and Serve:**
    - Let the quiche cool for at least 10 minutes before slicing. Serve warm or at room temperature.

## Tips:

- **Customize:** Feel free to add other spring vegetables like peas or leeks based on availability.
- **For a Flakier Crust:** Make sure the butter and water are very cold when making the dough.

Enjoy your Spring Herb Quiche—a delightful and fresh addition to any meal!

**Grilled Artichokes with Lemon Aioli**

## Ingredients:

**For the Artichokes:**

- **4 large artichokes**
- **2 lemons**, halved
- **3 cloves garlic**, minced
- **1/4 cup olive oil**
- **Salt and freshly ground black pepper**, to taste

**For the Lemon Aioli:**

- **1/2 cup mayonnaise**
- **2 tablespoons lemon juice**
- **1 clove garlic**, minced
- **1 teaspoon lemon zest**
- **1 tablespoon olive oil**
- **Salt and freshly ground black pepper**, to taste

## Instructions:

1. **Prepare the Artichokes:**
   - Fill a large bowl with water and squeeze the juice from one of the lemon halves into the water. This will prevent the artichokes from browning.
   - Trim the artichokes by cutting off the top third and removing any tough outer leaves. Cut the artichokes in half lengthwise and scoop out the fuzzy choke using a spoon.
   - Place the trimmed artichokes into the lemon water.
2. **Cook the Artichokes:**
   - Bring a large pot of salted water to a boil. Add the artichokes and cook for 10-15 minutes, until just tender. They should be easily pierced with a knife.
   - Drain and let cool slightly.
3. **Prepare the Aioli:**
   - In a small bowl, whisk together the mayonnaise, lemon juice, minced garlic, lemon zest, olive oil, salt, and pepper. Adjust seasoning to taste. Refrigerate until ready to use.
4. **Grill the Artichokes:**
   - Preheat your grill to medium-high heat.
   - Brush the artichokes with olive oil and season with salt and pepper.
   - Grill the artichokes cut side down for about 5-7 minutes, or until grill marks appear and the artichokes are heated through. Flip and grill for an additional 3-4 minutes, if desired.
5. **Serve:**
   - Serve the grilled artichokes warm with the lemon aioli on the side for dipping.

## Tips:

- **For Extra Flavor:** You can add herbs like rosemary or thyme to the water while boiling the artichokes for added aroma.

- **Garnish:** Sprinkle with a little extra lemon juice or fresh herbs before serving for added freshness.

Enjoy your Grilled Artichokes with Lemon Aioli—a delightful appetizer or side dish with a smoky, tangy twist!

**Chilled Cucumber Soup**

## Ingredients:

- **2 large cucumbers**, peeled and seeded
- **1/2 cup Greek yogurt**

- **1/4 cup sour cream** (optional for extra creaminess)
- **1/4 cup fresh dill**, chopped (or 1 tablespoon dried dill)
- **1 clove garlic**, minced
- **2 tablespoons lemon juice**
- **1 tablespoon olive oil**
- **Salt and freshly ground black pepper**, to taste
- **1/4 cup thinly sliced scallions** (optional, for garnish)
- **Additional fresh dill**, for garnish

## Instructions:

1. **Prepare the Cucumbers:**
   - Cut the cucumbers into chunks and place them in a blender or food processor.
2. **Blend the Soup:**
   - Add the Greek yogurt, sour cream (if using), fresh dill, garlic, lemon juice, olive oil, salt, and pepper to the blender.
   - Blend until smooth. If the soup is too thick, you can add a bit of water to reach your desired consistency.
3. **Chill:**
   - Transfer the soup to a bowl or container, cover, and refrigerate for at least 1 hour to allow the flavors to meld and the soup to chill.
4. **Serve:**
   - Stir the soup before serving. Garnish with thinly sliced scallions and additional fresh dill, if desired.

## Tips:

- **For Extra Texture:** Add some finely diced cucumber or a few croutons to the soup before serving for added crunch.
- **Flavor Variations:** Try adding a splash of white wine vinegar or a pinch of cayenne pepper for a different twist.

Enjoy your Chilled Cucumber Soup—it's a cool and refreshing option that's easy to prepare and perfect for hot days!

**Lemon Raspberry Muffins**

## Ingredients:

- 1 1/2 cups all-purpose flour
- 1/2 cup granulated sugar

- **1/4 cup brown sugar**, packed
- **1/2 teaspoon baking powder**
- **1/2 teaspoon baking soda**
- **1/4 teaspoon salt**
- **1/2 cup unsalted butter**, melted and slightly cooled
- **1 large egg**
- **1/2 cup milk** (whole milk or 2%)
- **1 tablespoon lemon zest** (about 1 lemon)
- **2 tablespoons fresh lemon juice**
- **1 teaspoon vanilla extract**
- **1 cup fresh raspberries** (or frozen, but do not thaw)

**For the Streusel Topping (optional):**

- **1/4 cup all-purpose flour**
- **2 tablespoons granulated sugar**
- **2 tablespoons unsalted butter**, cold and cut into small pieces
- **1/4 teaspoon ground cinnamon** (optional)

## Instructions:

1. **Preheat Oven:**
   - Preheat your oven to 375°F (190°C). Line a muffin tin with paper liners or lightly grease the cups.
2. **Prepare Dry Ingredients:**
   - In a large bowl, whisk together the flour, granulated sugar, brown sugar, baking powder, baking soda, and salt.
3. **Mix Wet Ingredients:**
   - In another bowl, whisk together the melted butter, egg, milk, lemon zest, lemon juice, and vanilla extract until well combined.
4. **Combine:**
   - Pour the wet ingredients into the dry ingredients and stir until just combined. Be careful not to overmix.
   - Gently fold in the raspberries. If using frozen raspberries, fold them in gently to prevent them from bleeding too much into the batter.
5. **Prepare the Streusel Topping (Optional):**
   - In a small bowl, mix the flour, sugar, and cinnamon. Cut in the cold butter using a fork or pastry cutter until the mixture resembles coarse crumbs. Sprinkle over the muffin batter if using.
6. **Fill Muffin Tin:**
   - Divide the batter evenly among the muffin cups, filling each about 3/4 full.
7. **Bake:**
   - Bake in the preheated oven for 20-25 minutes, or until a toothpick inserted into the center of a muffin comes out clean.
8. **Cool:**

- Allow the muffins to cool in the tin for 5 minutes, then transfer them to a wire rack to cool completely.

## Tips:

- **For Extra Moisture:** You can add a little more milk if the batter is too thick.
- **Lemon Glaze:** For a sweet touch, drizzle a lemon glaze (made from powdered sugar and lemon juice) over the muffins after they've cooled.

Enjoy your Lemon Raspberry Muffins—perfectly sweet, tangy, and bursting with fresh fruit flavor!

**Baked Stuffed Portobello Mushrooms**

## Ingredients:

- **4 large portobello mushrooms**, stems removed and gills scraped out

- **2 tablespoons olive oil**
- **1 small onion**, finely chopped
- **2 cloves garlic**, minced
- **1/2 cup breadcrumbs** (preferably whole wheat or panko)
- **1/4 cup grated Parmesan cheese**
- **1/4 cup chopped fresh parsley** (or 2 tablespoons dried parsley)
- **1/4 cup chopped sun-dried tomatoes** (optional)
- **1/4 cup chopped walnuts** or **pine nuts** (optional)
- **Salt and freshly ground black pepper**, to taste
- **1/2 teaspoon dried oregano** (or 1 teaspoon fresh oregano)
- **1/2 teaspoon dried basil** (or 1 teaspoon fresh basil)
- **1/2 cup shredded mozzarella cheese** (optional, for topping)

## Instructions:

1. **Preheat Oven:**
    - Preheat your oven to 375°F (190°C).
2. **Prepare the Mushrooms:**
    - Brush the portobello mushrooms with olive oil and season with salt and pepper. Place them gill-side up on a baking sheet.
3. **Prepare the Stuffing:**
    - Heat 1 tablespoon of olive oil in a skillet over medium heat. Add the chopped onion and cook until soft and translucent, about 5 minutes.
    - Add the minced garlic and cook for another 1 minute.
    - In a bowl, combine the cooked onion and garlic with breadcrumbs, Parmesan cheese, parsley, sun-dried tomatoes, walnuts (if using), oregano, basil, salt, and pepper.
4. **Stuff the Mushrooms:**
    - Spoon the stuffing mixture evenly into each portobello mushroom cap, pressing down slightly to pack the filling.
5. **Bake:**
    - Drizzle the remaining 1 tablespoon of olive oil over the stuffed mushrooms.
    - Bake in the preheated oven for 20-25 minutes, or until the mushrooms are tender and the stuffing is golden and crispy.
    - If using mozzarella cheese, sprinkle it on top of the stuffing in the last 5 minutes of baking, allowing it to melt and become bubbly.
6. **Serve:**
    - Let the stuffed mushrooms cool slightly before serving. They can be enjoyed warm or at room temperature.

## Tips:

- **For Extra Flavor:** Add chopped fresh herbs like thyme or rosemary to the stuffing.

- **Make Ahead:** The stuffed mushrooms can be assembled in advance and baked just before serving.

Enjoy your Baked Stuffed Portobello Mushrooms—a delicious and hearty option that's sure to impress!

**Thai Spring Rolls with Peanut Sauce**

## Ingredients:

**For the Spring Rolls:**

- **12 rice paper wrappers**
- **1 cup cooked rice noodles** (optional)
- **1 cup shredded lettuce** or **baby spinach**
- **1 cup shredded carrots**
- **1/2 cup cucumber**, julienned
- **1/2 cup red bell pepper**, julienned
- **1/4 cup fresh mint leaves**
- **1/4 cup fresh cilantro leaves**
- **1/4 cup fresh basil leaves**
- **1/2 cup cooked shrimp** (optional), sliced in half lengthwise

**For the Peanut Sauce:**

- **1/4 cup peanut butter**
- **2 tablespoons soy sauce**
- **1 tablespoon hoisin sauce**
- **1 tablespoon rice vinegar**
- **1 tablespoon honey** or **maple syrup**
- **1 clove garlic**, minced
- **1/2 teaspoon grated fresh ginger**
- **Water**, as needed to thin the sauce

## Instructions:

1. **Prepare the Ingredients:**
   - Cook the rice noodles according to the package instructions. Rinse under cold water and drain.
   - Prepare and slice all the vegetables and herbs. If using shrimp, cook and slice them.
2. **Make the Peanut Sauce:**
   - In a bowl, whisk together the peanut butter, soy sauce, hoisin sauce, rice vinegar, honey, minced garlic, and grated ginger.
   - Add water a little at a time until the sauce reaches your desired consistency. It should be smooth and slightly thick but pourable.
3. **Assemble the Spring Rolls:**
   - Fill a large shallow dish or plate with warm water. Dip one rice paper wrapper into the water for about 10-15 seconds, or until it becomes pliable but not too soft.
   - Lay the wrapper flat on a clean surface. Place a small amount of lettuce (or spinach), rice noodles (if using), shredded carrots, cucumber, red bell pepper, mint, cilantro, basil, and a few shrimp (if using) in the center of the wrapper.

- Fold the sides of the wrapper over the filling, then roll from the bottom up, tucking in the sides as you go to make a tight roll. Repeat with the remaining wrappers and filling.
4. **Serve:**
    - Arrange the spring rolls on a serving platter. Serve with the peanut sauce for dipping.

## Tips:

- **For a Crunchier Texture:** Add some sliced cabbage or bean sprouts to the filling.
- **Make Ahead:** The spring rolls can be made a few hours in advance and stored covered in the refrigerator.

Enjoy your Thai Spring Rolls with Peanut Sauce—fresh, flavorful, and perfect for any occasion!

**Fennel and Apple Salad**

## Ingredients:

- **1 large fennel bulb**, thinly sliced
- **2 apples**, thinly sliced (such as Fuji or Granny Smith)
- **1/4 cup red onion**, thinly sliced
- **2 tablespoons fresh lemon juice**
- **3 tablespoons olive oil**
- **1 teaspoon honey** or **maple syrup**
- **Salt and freshly ground black pepper**, to taste
- **1/4 cup chopped fresh parsley** or **fresh dill** (optional)
- **1/4 cup crumbled feta cheese** or **toasted nuts** (optional, for garnish)

## Instructions:

1. **Prepare the Vegetables and Fruit:**
   - Thinly slice the fennel bulb, apples, and red onion. If you prefer, you can use a mandoline for even slices.
2. **Make the Dressing:**
   - In a small bowl, whisk together the lemon juice, olive oil, honey (or maple syrup), salt, and pepper until well combined.
3. **Assemble the Salad:**
   - In a large bowl, combine the fennel, apple slices, and red onion.
   - Pour the dressing over the salad and toss gently to coat.
4. **Garnish and Serve:**
   - Garnish with chopped parsley or dill, and top with crumbled feta cheese or toasted nuts if desired.
   - Serve immediately or chill for 10-15 minutes to let the flavors meld.

## Tips:

- **For Extra Crunch:** Add some thinly sliced celery or radishes.
- **Make Ahead:** The salad can be prepared a few hours in advance but is best enjoyed fresh to maintain its crisp texture.

Enjoy your Fennel and Apple Salad—crisp, refreshing, and perfect for any meal!

**Roasted Vegetable Medley**

## Ingredients:

- **1 red bell pepper**, chopped
- **1 yellow bell pepper**, chopped
- **1 zucchini**, sliced
- **1 red onion**, chopped
- **1 cup cherry tomatoes**, halved
- **2 carrots**, sliced
- **2 tablespoons olive oil**
- **1 teaspoon dried oregano**
- **1 teaspoon dried thyme**
- **1/2 teaspoon garlic powder**
- **Salt and freshly ground black pepper**, to taste
- **Fresh basil or parsley**, for garnish (optional)

## Instructions:

1. **Preheat Oven:**
   - Preheat your oven to 425°F (220°C).
2. **Prepare Vegetables:**
   - In a large bowl, combine the chopped bell peppers, zucchini, red onion, cherry tomatoes, and carrots.
3. **Season and Toss:**
   - Drizzle the olive oil over the vegetables. Add the oregano, thyme, garlic powder, salt, and pepper. Toss everything together until the vegetables are evenly coated.
4. **Roast:**
   - Spread the vegetables in a single layer on a baking sheet. Roast in the preheated oven for 25-30 minutes, or until the vegetables are tender and slightly caramelized, stirring halfway through.
5. **Garnish and Serve:**
   - Remove from the oven and let cool slightly. Garnish with fresh basil or parsley if desired.

## Tips:

- **For Extra Flavor:** Add a splash of balsamic vinegar or a sprinkle of Parmesan cheese before serving.
- **Mix and Match:** Feel free to use any seasonal vegetables you have on hand, such as sweet potatoes, butternut squash, or Brussels sprouts.

Enjoy your Roasted Vegetable Medley—a versatile and delicious side dish that's easy to make and full of flavor!

**Herb-Crusted Chicken Breasts**

## Ingredients:

- **4 boneless, skinless chicken breasts**
- **1/2 cup breadcrumbs** (preferably panko for extra crunch)
- **1/4 cup grated Parmesan cheese**
- **2 tablespoons fresh parsley**, chopped (or 1 tablespoon dried parsley)
- **1 tablespoon fresh thyme leaves** (or 1 teaspoon dried thyme)
- **1 tablespoon fresh rosemary**, chopped (or 1 teaspoon dried rosemary)
- **1/2 teaspoon garlic powder**
- **1/2 teaspoon onion powder**
- **Salt and freshly ground black pepper**, to taste
- **1/4 cup Dijon mustard**
- **2 tablespoons olive oil**

## Instructions:

1. **Preheat Oven:**
   - Preheat your oven to 400°F (200°C).
2. **Prepare the Herb Coating:**
   - In a shallow dish, combine the breadcrumbs, Parmesan cheese, parsley, thyme, rosemary, garlic powder, onion powder, salt, and pepper.
3. **Prepare the Chicken:**
   - Season the chicken breasts with salt and pepper.
   - Brush each chicken breast with Dijon mustard, which will help the herb coating adhere better.
4. **Coat the Chicken:**
   - Dredge each mustard-coated chicken breast in the herb mixture, pressing lightly to ensure the coating sticks.
5. **Cook the Chicken:**
   - Heat olive oil in a large ovenproof skillet over medium-high heat. Add the chicken breasts and cook for 2-3 minutes per side, or until the coating is golden brown.
   - Transfer the skillet to the preheated oven and bake for 15-20 minutes, or until the chicken reaches an internal temperature of 165°F (74°C) and is cooked through.
6. **Serve:**
   - Let the chicken rest for 5 minutes before slicing. Serve with your favorite side dishes.

## Tips:

- **For Extra Crunch:** Add a tablespoon of finely chopped nuts to the herb mixture.
- **Make Ahead:** The herb-coated chicken can be prepared in advance and refrigerated until ready to cook.

Enjoy your Herb-Crusted Chicken Breasts—a flavorful and crispy dish that's perfect for any occasion!

**Strawberry Rhubarb Crisp**

## Ingredients:

**For the Filling:**

- **3 cups fresh strawberries**, hulled and sliced
- **3 cups fresh rhubarb**, chopped into 1/2-inch pieces
- **1 cup granulated sugar**
- **2 tablespoons cornstarch**
- **1 tablespoon lemon juice**
- **1/2 teaspoon vanilla extract**

**For the Topping:**

- **1 cup rolled oats**
- **1/2 cup all-purpose flour**
- **1/2 cup packed brown sugar**
- **1/2 teaspoon ground cinnamon**
- **1/4 teaspoon salt**
- **1/2 cup unsalted butter**, cold and cut into small pieces

## Instructions:

1. **Preheat Oven:**
   - Preheat your oven to 375°F (190°C).
2. **Prepare the Filling:**
   - In a large bowl, combine the strawberries, rhubarb, granulated sugar, cornstarch, lemon juice, and vanilla extract. Toss until well mixed.
   - Pour the filling into a 9x13-inch baking dish or a similar-sized ovenproof dish.
3. **Prepare the Topping:**
   - In a medium bowl, mix together the oats, flour, brown sugar, cinnamon, and salt.
   - Add the cold butter pieces and use your fingers or a pastry cutter to work the butter into the dry ingredients until the mixture resembles coarse crumbs.
4. **Assemble and Bake:**
   - Sprinkle the topping evenly over the fruit filling.
   - Bake in the preheated oven for 40-45 minutes, or until the topping is golden brown and the filling is bubbly.
5. **Cool and Serve:**
   - Let the crisp cool slightly before serving. It's delicious on its own or topped with a scoop of vanilla ice cream or a dollop of whipped cream.

## Tips:

- **For Extra Crunch:** Add a handful of chopped nuts to the topping mixture.

- **Make Ahead:** The crisp can be prepared a day in advance and stored covered at room temperature.

Enjoy your Strawberry Rhubarb Crisp—a perfect blend of sweet and tart with a delightful crunch!

**Arugula and Parmesan Salad**

## Ingredients:

- **4 cups fresh arugula**
- **1/4 cup shaved Parmesan cheese**
- **1/4 cup pine nuts** or **walnuts**, toasted
- **1/4 cup extra virgin olive oil**
- **2 tablespoons fresh lemon juice**
- **1 teaspoon Dijon mustard**
- **Salt and freshly ground black pepper**, to taste

## Instructions:

1. **Prepare the Salad:**
    - Place the arugula in a large salad bowl.
2. **Make the Dressing:**
    - In a small bowl, whisk together the olive oil, lemon juice, Dijon mustard, salt, and pepper until well combined.
3. **Assemble the Salad:**
    - Drizzle the dressing over the arugula and toss gently to coat.
    - Top with shaved Parmesan and toasted pine nuts or walnuts.
4. **Serve:**
    - Serve immediately for the freshest taste.

## Tips:

- **For Extra Flavor:** Add a few slices of thinly shaved red onion or a handful of cherry tomatoes.
- **Make Ahead:** Prepare the salad ingredients and dressing separately, then combine just before serving to keep the arugula crisp.

Enjoy your Arugula and Parmesan Salad—fresh, simple, and full of flavor!

**Lemon Blueberry Scones**

## Ingredients:

**For the Scones:**

- **2 cups all-purpose flour**
- **1/4 cup granulated sugar**
- **1 tablespoon baking powder**
- **1/2 teaspoon salt**
- **1/2 cup cold unsalted butter**, cut into small pieces
- **1 cup fresh blueberries** (or frozen, but do not thaw)
- **1/2 cup whole milk** or **heavy cream**
- **1 large egg**
- **1 tablespoon lemon zest** (about 1 lemon)
- **1 tablespoon fresh lemon juice**

**For the Glaze (optional):**

- **1/2 cup powdered sugar**
- **1-2 tablespoons lemon juice**
- **1/2 teaspoon lemon zest**

## Instructions:

1. **Preheat Oven:**
   - Preheat your oven to 400°F (200°C). Line a baking sheet with parchment paper.
2. **Prepare the Scone Dough:**
   - In a large bowl, whisk together the flour, sugar, baking powder, and salt.
   - Add the cold butter pieces. Use a pastry cutter, two forks, or your fingers to cut the butter into the flour mixture until it resembles coarse crumbs.
   - Gently fold in the blueberries.
   - In a separate bowl, whisk together the milk, egg, lemon zest, and lemon juice.
   - Add the wet ingredients to the dry ingredients and stir until just combined. Be careful not to overmix.
3. **Shape and Cut the Scones:**
   - Turn the dough out onto a lightly floured surface and gently knead a few times to bring it together.
   - Pat the dough into a 1-inch thick circle. Using a knife or a pizza cutter, cut the dough into 8 wedges or use a round cutter to make individual scones.
   - Transfer the scones to the prepared baking sheet, spacing them about 2 inches apart.
4. **Bake:**
   - Bake in the preheated oven for 15-18 minutes, or until the scones are golden brown on top.

5. **Make the Glaze (Optional):**
    - While the scones are baking, whisk together the powdered sugar, lemon juice, and lemon zest in a small bowl. Adjust the consistency with more lemon juice or powdered sugar as needed.
6. **Glaze and Serve:**
    - Allow the scones to cool slightly before drizzling with the lemon glaze.
    - Serve warm or at room temperature.

## Tips:

- **For Extra Moisture:** If using frozen blueberries, toss them in a little flour before adding to the dough to help prevent bleeding.
- **Customize:** You can add a handful of chopped nuts or a sprinkle of coarse sugar on top of the scones before baking for added texture.

Enjoy your Lemon Blueberry Scones—a perfect combination of tangy lemon and sweet blueberries in a buttery, flaky treat!

**Creamy Polenta with Roasted Tomatoes**

## Ingredients:

**For the Polenta:**

- **1 cup polenta (cornmeal)**
- **4 cups water or vegetable broth**
- **1/2 cup grated Parmesan cheese**
- **2 tablespoons unsalted butter**
- **Salt and freshly ground black pepper**, to taste

**For the Roasted Tomatoes:**

- **2 cups cherry or grape tomatoes**, halved
- **2 tablespoons olive oil**
- **1 tablespoon balsamic vinegar**
- **1 teaspoon dried oregano** or **thyme**
- **Salt and freshly ground black pepper**, to taste

## Instructions:

1. **Roast the Tomatoes:**
    - Preheat your oven to 400°F (200°C).
    - In a bowl, toss the tomatoes with olive oil, balsamic vinegar, oregano (or thyme), salt, and pepper.
    - Spread the tomatoes on a baking sheet in a single layer.
    - Roast for 20-25 minutes, or until the tomatoes are caramelized and slightly wrinkled.
2. **Prepare the Polenta:**
    - In a large pot, bring the water or vegetable broth to a boil.
    - Gradually whisk in the polenta to avoid lumps.
    - Reduce the heat to low and cook, stirring frequently, for 25-30 minutes, or until the polenta is thick and creamy.
    - Stir in the Parmesan cheese and butter. Season with salt and pepper to taste.
3. **Serve:**
    - Spoon the creamy polenta onto plates or a serving dish.
    - Top with the roasted tomatoes.
    - Garnish with extra Parmesan cheese or fresh herbs if desired.

## Tips:

- **For Extra Flavor:** Stir in some fresh basil or a drizzle of extra balsamic vinegar before serving.

- **Make Ahead:** Both the polenta and roasted tomatoes can be prepared in advance and reheated.

Enjoy your Creamy Polenta with Roasted Tomatoes—a creamy, flavorful dish that's both comforting and satisfying!

**Grilled Veggie Wraps**

## Ingredients:

- **4 large tortillas** (whole wheat, flour, or your choice)
- **1 red bell pepper**, sliced
- **1 yellow bell pepper**, sliced
- **1 zucchini**, sliced
- **1 small eggplant**, sliced
- **1 red onion**, sliced
- **2 tablespoons olive oil**
- **1 teaspoon dried oregano**
- **Salt and freshly ground black pepper**, to taste
- **1/2 cup hummus** (store-bought or homemade)
- **1 cup baby spinach** or **mixed greens**
- **1/2 cup crumbled feta cheese** or **shredded cheese** (optional)
- **1 tablespoon balsamic glaze** (optional)

## Instructions:

1. **Prepare the Vegetables:**
   - Preheat your grill or grill pan to medium-high heat.
   - In a large bowl, toss the sliced bell peppers, zucchini, eggplant, and red onion with olive oil, oregano, salt, and pepper.
2. **Grill the Vegetables:**
   - Grill the vegetables for 3-5 minutes per side, or until tender and slightly charred. Remove from the grill and let cool slightly.
3. **Assemble the Wraps:**
   - Spread a layer of hummus over each tortilla.
   - Arrange the grilled vegetables evenly on the tortillas.
   - Top with baby spinach, crumbled feta cheese, and a drizzle of balsamic glaze if using.
4. **Wrap and Serve:**
   - Roll up each tortilla tightly, tucking in the sides as you go.
   - Slice in half diagonally if desired.

## Tips:

- **For Extra Crunch:** Add some sliced cucumbers or shredded carrots.
- **Make Ahead:** The grilled vegetables can be prepared a day in advance and stored in the refrigerator.

Enjoy your Grilled Veggie Wraps—a flavorful and nutritious option for a quick and satisfying meal!

**Poached Eggs with Asparagus**

## Ingredients:

- **8 asparagus spears**, trimmed
- **4 large eggs**
- **1 tablespoon white vinegar** (for poaching)
- **Salt and freshly ground black pepper**, to taste
- **1 tablespoon olive oil** (optional, for drizzling)
- **1 tablespoon fresh lemon juice** (optional, for added flavor)
- **Chopped fresh parsley** or **chives**, for garnish (optional)

## Instructions:

1. **Prepare the Asparagus:**
   - Bring a pot of salted water to a boil.
   - Add the asparagus and cook for 2-3 minutes, or until tender-crisp. Drain and immediately transfer the asparagus to a bowl of ice water to stop the cooking. Drain again and pat dry.
2. **Poach the Eggs:**
   - Fill a medium pot with water and add the white vinegar. Bring to a simmer over medium heat.
   - Crack one egg into a small bowl. Create a gentle whirlpool in the simmering water by stirring with a spoon. Carefully slide the egg into the center of the whirlpool. Cook for 3-4 minutes, or until the white is set but the yolk is still runny.
   - Remove the egg with a slotted spoon and transfer to a plate. Repeat with the remaining eggs.
3. **Serve:**
   - Arrange the asparagus on serving plates.
   - Top with poached eggs.
   - Season with salt and pepper. Drizzle with olive oil and lemon juice if desired.
   - Garnish with fresh parsley or chives.

## Tips:

- **For Extra Flavor:** Add a sprinkle of Parmesan cheese or a pinch of red pepper flakes.
- **Poaching Tip:** Use very fresh eggs for the best results, as they hold their shape better when poached.

Enjoy your Poached Eggs with Asparagus—a simple yet elegant dish that's perfect for a special breakfast or brunch!

**Spring Onion and Potato Soup**

## Ingredients:

- **1 tablespoon olive oil**
- **1 large onion**, diced
- **4-5 spring onions**, sliced (white and green parts separated)
- **3 cloves garlic**, minced
- **4 cups vegetable or chicken broth**
- **4 medium potatoes**, peeled and diced
- **1 cup milk** or **cream**
- **Salt and freshly ground black pepper**, to taste
- **1 tablespoon fresh thyme** or **dried thyme**
- **1 tablespoon chopped fresh parsley** (optional, for garnish)

## Instructions:

1. **Sauté the Vegetables:**
   - Heat the olive oil in a large pot over medium heat.
   - Add the diced onion and cook until softened, about 5 minutes.
   - Add the sliced spring onions (white parts) and garlic. Cook for another 2 minutes until fragrant.
2. **Cook the Potatoes:**
   - Add the diced potatoes to the pot and stir to combine with the onions.
   - Pour in the broth and add the thyme. Bring to a boil, then reduce heat and simmer for 15-20 minutes, or until the potatoes are tender.
3. **Blend the Soup:**
   - Use an immersion blender to blend the soup until smooth. Alternatively, carefully transfer the soup in batches to a countertop blender.
4. **Finish the Soup:**
   - Stir in the milk or cream and season with salt and pepper to taste.
   - Heat through until warmed.
5. **Serve:**
   - Ladle the soup into bowls.
   - Garnish with the green parts of the spring onions and chopped parsley if desired.

## Tips:

- **For Extra Creaminess:** Substitute some of the milk with additional cream or use a bit of sour cream.
- **Add Texture:** Garnish with croutons or a sprinkle of shredded cheese.

Enjoy your Spring Onion and Potato Soup—a rich, smooth, and comforting dish that's easy to prepare and perfect for any meal!

**Watermelon and Feta Salad**

## Ingredients:

- **4 cups watermelon**, cubed
- **1 cup crumbled feta cheese**
- **1/4 cup fresh mint leaves**, chopped
- **1/4 cup red onion**, thinly sliced (optional)
- **2 tablespoons extra virgin olive oil**
- **1 tablespoon balsamic vinegar** or **lime juice**
- **Salt and freshly ground black pepper**, to taste
- **1 tablespoon honey** or **agave syrup** (optional, for a touch of sweetness)

## Instructions:

1. **Prepare the Ingredients:**
   - Cube the watermelon and crumble the feta cheese. Chop the fresh mint leaves.
2. **Assemble the Salad:**
   - In a large bowl, combine the watermelon, feta cheese, and chopped mint. If using, add the thinly sliced red onion.
3. **Make the Dressing:**
   - In a small bowl, whisk together the olive oil, balsamic vinegar (or lime juice), salt, pepper, and honey (if using).
4. **Dress and Toss:**
   - Drizzle the dressing over the salad and toss gently to combine.
5. **Serve:**
   - Serve immediately or chill for 10-15 minutes to let the flavors meld.

## Tips:

- **For Extra Crunch:** Add some toasted pine nuts or slivers of almonds.
- **Add Protein:** Toss in some grilled chicken or shrimp for a heartier meal.

Enjoy your Watermelon and Feta Salad—a perfect blend of sweet, tangy, and refreshing flavors!

**Honey Mustard Glazed Carrots**

## Ingredients:

- **1 lb (450g) carrots**, peeled and cut into bite-sized pieces
- **2 tablespoons olive oil**
- **2 tablespoons honey**
- **2 tablespoons Dijon mustard**
- **1 tablespoon whole grain mustard** (optional, for extra texture)
- **Salt and freshly ground black pepper**, to taste
- **1 tablespoon fresh parsley**, chopped (optional, for garnish)

## Instructions:

1. **Preheat Oven:**
    - Preheat your oven to 425°F (220°C). Line a baking sheet with parchment paper.
2. **Prepare the Carrots:**
    - Toss the carrot pieces with olive oil, salt, and pepper. Spread them out in a single layer on the prepared baking sheet.
3. **Roast the Carrots:**
    - Roast in the preheated oven for 20-25 minutes, or until tender and slightly caramelized, stirring halfway through.
4. **Prepare the Glaze:**
    - While the carrots are roasting, in a small bowl, whisk together the honey, Dijon mustard, and whole grain mustard (if using).
5. **Glaze the Carrots:**
    - Once the carrots are done roasting, remove them from the oven.
    - Drizzle the honey mustard glaze over the carrots and toss to coat evenly.
6. **Serve:**
    - Garnish with chopped parsley if desired and serve warm.

## Tips:

- **For Extra Flavor:** Add a pinch of smoked paprika or a squeeze of lemon juice.
- **Make Ahead:** The glaze can be made in advance and stored in the refrigerator.

Enjoy your Honey Mustard Glazed Carrots—sweet, tangy, and perfect for any meal!

**Sautéed Shrimp with Lemon and Garlic**

## Ingredients:

- **1 lb (450g) large shrimp**, peeled and deveined
- **2 tablespoons olive oil**
- **4 cloves garlic**, minced
- **Zest and juice of 1 lemon**
- **Salt and freshly ground black pepper**, to taste
- **1/4 teaspoon red pepper flakes** (optional, for a bit of heat)
- **2 tablespoons fresh parsley**, chopped (optional, for garnish)

## Instructions:

1. **Heat the Oil:**
   - In a large skillet, heat the olive oil over medium-high heat.
2. **Sauté the Shrimp:**
   - Add the shrimp to the skillet in a single layer. Cook for 1-2 minutes on each side, or until they turn pink and opaque.
3. **Add Garlic and Lemon:**
   - Add the minced garlic to the skillet and cook for an additional 30 seconds, or until fragrant.
   - Stir in the lemon zest and juice, and season with salt, pepper, and red pepper flakes if using.
4. **Finish and Serve:**
   - Remove from heat and garnish with fresh parsley if desired.
   - Serve immediately over pasta, rice, or with crusty bread.

## Tips:

- **For Extra Flavor:** Add a splash of white wine or a sprinkle of capers.
- **Cooking Time:** Be careful not to overcook the shrimp, as they can become tough.

Enjoy your Sautéed Shrimp with Lemon and Garlic—quick, flavorful, and perfect for a weeknight meal!

**Citrus Roasted Chicken**

## Ingredients:

- **1 whole chicken** (about 4-5 lbs)
- **2 tablespoons olive oil**
- **1 lemon**, cut into wedges
- **1 orange**, cut into wedges
- **4 cloves garlic**, minced
- **2 teaspoons dried thyme** or **1 tablespoon fresh thyme**
- **1 teaspoon dried rosemary** or **1 tablespoon fresh rosemary**
- **Salt and freshly ground black pepper**, to taste
- **1/2 cup chicken broth** or **white wine** (for basting)
- **1 tablespoon honey** (optional, for added sweetness)

## Instructions:

1. **Preheat Oven:**
   - Preheat your oven to 425°F (220°C).
2. **Prepare the Chicken:**
   - Pat the chicken dry with paper towels. Rub the outside and inside of the chicken with olive oil.
   - Season generously with salt, pepper, thyme, and rosemary.
3. **Stuff the Chicken:**
   - Stuff the cavity of the chicken with the lemon and orange wedges, and a few garlic cloves.
4. **Roast the Chicken:**
   - Place the chicken breast-side up on a rack in a roasting pan. Pour the chicken broth or white wine into the bottom of the pan.
   - Roast for 1-1.5 hours, or until the internal temperature reaches 165°F (74°C) and the skin is golden and crispy. Baste occasionally with the pan juices.
5. **Optional Glaze:**
   - If desired, mix honey with a little water and brush over the chicken during the last 15 minutes of roasting for a slight glaze.
6. **Rest and Serve:**
   - Let the chicken rest for 10-15 minutes before carving.

## Tips:

- **For Extra Flavor:** Add additional herbs or citrus slices under the skin or in the roasting pan.
- **Make Ahead:** The chicken can be seasoned and stuffed a day in advance and kept in the refrigerator.

Enjoy your Citrus Roasted Chicken—a flavorful and juicy dish with a bright citrus twist!

**Artichoke and Spinach Dip**

## Ingredients:

- **1 can (14 oz) artichoke hearts**, drained and chopped
- **1 cup fresh spinach**, chopped (or **1 cup frozen spinach**, thawed and squeezed dry)
- **1 cup sour cream**
- **1 cup mayonnaise**
- **1 cup grated Parmesan cheese**
- **1 cup shredded mozzarella cheese**
- **2 cloves garlic**, minced
- **1/2 teaspoon onion powder**
- **1/2 teaspoon dried basil** or **1 tablespoon fresh basil**, chopped
- **Salt and freshly ground black pepper**, to taste
- **1/2 teaspoon red pepper flakes** (optional, for a bit of heat)

## Instructions:

1. **Preheat Oven:**
   - Preheat your oven to 375°F (190°C).
2. **Mix the Ingredients:**
   - In a large bowl, combine the chopped artichoke hearts, spinach, sour cream, mayonnaise, Parmesan cheese, mozzarella cheese, garlic, onion powder, basil, salt, pepper, and red pepper flakes if using.
3. **Bake the Dip:**
   - Transfer the mixture to a baking dish (about 8x8 inches or similar).
   - Bake for 25-30 minutes, or until the dip is hot and bubbly and the top is golden brown.
4. **Serve:**
   - Serve warm with sliced baguette, pita chips, tortilla chips, or fresh vegetable sticks.

## Tips:

- **For Extra Crunch:** Top the dip with a bit more Parmesan cheese or breadcrumbs before baking.
- **Make Ahead:** The dip can be assembled a day in advance and stored in the refrigerator. Just bake before serving.

Enjoy your Artichoke and Spinach Dip—a creamy, cheesy treat that's always a crowd-pleaser!

**Cherry Tomato and Basil Bruschetta**

## Ingredients:

- **1 pint cherry tomatoes**, halved
- **1/4 cup fresh basil leaves**, chopped
- **2 tablespoons extra virgin olive oil**
- **1 tablespoon balsamic vinegar**
- **1 clove garlic**, minced
- **Salt and freshly ground black pepper**, to taste
- **1 baguette**, sliced into 1/2-inch pieces
- **1/4 cup grated Parmesan cheese** (optional, for serving)

## Instructions:

1. **Prepare the Tomato Mixture:**
   - In a medium bowl, combine the cherry tomatoes, chopped basil, olive oil, balsamic vinegar, minced garlic, salt, and pepper. Toss gently to mix.
2. **Toast the Baguette:**
   - Preheat your oven to 400°F (200°C).
   - Arrange the baguette slices on a baking sheet. Toast in the oven for 5-7 minutes, or until lightly golden and crisp.
3. **Assemble the Bruschetta:**
   - Spoon the tomato mixture onto the toasted baguette slices.
   - If desired, sprinkle with grated Parmesan cheese.
4. **Serve:**
   - Serve immediately for the best texture and flavor.

## Tips:

- **For Extra Flavor:** Add a drizzle of balsamic glaze or a sprinkle of red pepper flakes.
- **Make Ahead:** The tomato mixture can be prepared a few hours in advance and stored in the refrigerator. Toast the baguette slices just before serving.

Enjoy your Cherry Tomato and Basil Bruschetta—fresh, flavorful, and perfect for any occasion!

**Sweet Pea and Ricotta Crostini**

## Ingredients:

- **1 baguette**, sliced into 1/2-inch pieces
- **1 cup fresh peas** (or frozen peas, thawed)
- **1 cup ricotta cheese**
- **2 tablespoons extra virgin olive oil**, plus more for drizzling
- **1 clove garlic**, minced
- **Zest and juice of 1 lemon**
- **Salt and freshly ground black pepper**, to taste
- **1 tablespoon fresh mint or basil**, chopped (optional, for garnish)

## Instructions:

1. **Prepare the Crostini:**
    - Preheat your oven to 400°F (200°C).
    - Arrange the baguette slices on a baking sheet. Brush lightly with olive oil.
    - Toast in the oven for 5-7 minutes, or until the slices are golden brown and crisp. Remove from the oven and let cool.
2. **Prepare the Peas:**
    - If using fresh peas, blanch them in boiling water for 2 minutes, then transfer to an ice bath to cool. Drain and pat dry. If using frozen peas, just thaw them.
    - In a small bowl, toss the peas with a little olive oil, salt, and pepper. Optionally, you can lightly mash them with a fork for a more textured topping.
3. **Prepare the Ricotta Spread:**
    - In a medium bowl, mix the ricotta cheese with minced garlic, lemon zest, and lemon juice. Season with salt and pepper to taste.
4. **Assemble the Crostini:**
    - Spread a generous layer of the ricotta mixture onto each toasted baguette slice.
    - Top with the prepared peas.
    - Drizzle with a little more olive oil and garnish with chopped fresh mint or basil if desired.
5. **Serve:**
    - Serve immediately for the freshest taste.

## Tips:

- **For Extra Flavor:** Add a sprinkle of crushed red pepper flakes or a drizzle of honey for a sweet touch.
- **Make Ahead:** Prepare the ricotta spread and peas a few hours in advance. Assemble the crostini just before serving to keep them crisp.

Enjoy your Sweet Pea and Ricotta Crostini—a fresh, creamy, and delightful appetizer perfect for any occasion!

**Lemon Dill Baked Cod**

## Ingredients:

- **4 cod fillets** (about 6 oz each)
- **2 tablespoons olive oil**
- **2 tablespoons fresh lemon juice** (about 1 lemon)
- **2 teaspoons lemon zest** (about 1 lemon)
- **2 cloves garlic**, minced
- **2 tablespoons fresh dill**, chopped (or 1 tablespoon dried dill)
- **Salt and freshly ground black pepper**, to taste
- **Lemon wedges**, for serving

## Instructions:

1. **Preheat Oven:**
   - Preheat your oven to 400°F (200°C). Line a baking sheet with parchment paper or lightly grease it.
2. **Prepare the Cod:**
   - Place the cod fillets on the prepared baking sheet. Pat them dry with paper towels.
3. **Make the Lemon Dill Mixture:**
   - In a small bowl, combine the olive oil, lemon juice, lemon zest, minced garlic, chopped dill, salt, and pepper. Mix well.
4. **Season the Cod:**
   - Brush the lemon dill mixture evenly over the cod fillets.
5. **Bake:**
   - Bake the cod in the preheated oven for 12-15 minutes, or until the fish is opaque and flakes easily with a fork.
6. **Serve:**
   - Serve the baked cod with lemon wedges for additional freshness.

## Tips:

- **For Extra Flavor:** Add a sprinkle of paprika or a few capers before baking.
- **Check Doneness:** The cod is done when its internal temperature reaches 145°F (63°C).

Enjoy your Lemon Dill Baked Cod—light, zesty, and perfectly baked!

**Cauliflower Rice Stir-Fry**

## Ingredients:

- **1 head cauliflower**, grated or processed into rice-sized pieces
- **2 tablespoons olive oil** or **sesame oil**
- **1 cup mixed vegetables** (e.g., bell peppers, carrots, peas, corn), chopped
- **2 cloves garlic**, minced
- **1 tablespoon fresh ginger**, minced
- **2 tablespoons soy sauce** or **tamari** (for gluten-free)
- **1 tablespoon hoisin sauce** or **teriyaki sauce** (optional)
- **2 green onions**, chopped
- **1/2 cup cooked chicken, beef, or tofu** (optional, for added protein)
- **Salt and freshly ground black pepper**, to taste
- **1 teaspoon sesame seeds** (optional, for garnish)

## Instructions:

1. **Prepare the Cauliflower Rice:**
   - In a food processor, pulse the cauliflower florets until they resemble rice grains. Set aside.
2. **Cook the Vegetables:**
   - Heat the olive oil or sesame oil in a large skillet or wok over medium-high heat.
   - Add the garlic and ginger, cooking for about 30 seconds until fragrant.
   - Add the mixed vegetables and cook for 3-4 minutes, or until they start to soften.
3. **Add Cauliflower Rice:**
   - Stir in the cauliflower rice and cook for an additional 5-7 minutes, or until the cauliflower is tender and slightly golden.
4. **Season the Stir-Fry:**
   - Add the soy sauce and hoisin or teriyaki sauce if using. Stir well to combine.
   - Add the cooked protein (if using) and cook until heated through.
5. **Finish and Serve:**
   - Season with salt and pepper to taste.
   - Garnish with chopped green onions and sesame seeds if desired.

## Tips:

- **For Extra Flavor:** Add a splash of rice vinegar or a sprinkle of red pepper flakes.
- **Make Ahead:** The cauliflower rice and vegetable mixture can be prepared in advance and stored in the refrigerator.

Enjoy your Cauliflower Rice Stir-Fry—a healthy, quick, and versatile dish that's perfect for any meal!

**Apricot Glazed Chicken**

## Ingredients:

- **4 boneless, skinless chicken breasts** (or thighs)
- **1 cup apricot preserves** or **jam**
- **2 tablespoons Dijon mustard**
- **1 tablespoon soy sauce** or **tamari** (for gluten-free)
- **2 cloves garlic**, minced
- **1 tablespoon fresh ginger**, minced (optional)
- **1 tablespoon olive oil**
- **Salt and freshly ground black pepper**, to taste
- **Chopped fresh parsley** or **green onions**, for garnish (optional)

## Instructions:

1. **Preheat Oven:**
   - Preheat your oven to 375°F (190°C). Lightly grease a baking dish.
2. **Prepare the Glaze:**
   - In a small saucepan, combine the apricot preserves, Dijon mustard, soy sauce, minced garlic, and fresh ginger (if using).
   - Cook over medium heat, stirring occasionally, until the glaze is warmed through and slightly thickened, about 5 minutes. Set aside.
3. **Prepare the Chicken:**
   - Season the chicken breasts with salt and pepper.
   - Heat olive oil in a large skillet over medium-high heat. Sear the chicken breasts for 2-3 minutes per side, until lightly browned.
4. **Bake the Chicken:**
   - Transfer the seared chicken breasts to the prepared baking dish.
   - Brush or spoon the apricot glaze generously over each piece of chicken.
5. **Finish Baking:**
   - Bake in the preheated oven for 20-25 minutes, or until the chicken is cooked through and reaches an internal temperature of 165°F (74°C). Baste with the glaze halfway through cooking if desired.
6. **Serve:**
   - Garnish with chopped parsley or green onions if desired.
   - Serve with rice, quinoa, or a fresh vegetable side.

## Tips:

- **For Extra Glaze:** Make extra apricot glaze to drizzle over the chicken when serving or use it as a dipping sauce.
- **Add a Crunch:** Top with toasted almonds or sesame seeds for added texture.

Enjoy your Apricot Glazed Chicken—sweet, tangy, and perfectly baked!

**Radish and Herb Butter Spread**

## Ingredients:

- **1 cup unsalted butter**, softened
- **1 bunch radishes**, finely grated or chopped
- **2 tablespoons fresh chives**, chopped
- **2 tablespoons fresh parsley**, chopped
- **1 tablespoon fresh dill**, chopped (optional)
- **1 clove garlic**, minced (optional)
- **1 teaspoon lemon juice** or **white wine vinegar**
- **Salt and freshly ground black pepper**, to taste

## Instructions:

1. **Prepare the Radishes:**
   - Wash and trim the radishes. Grate or finely chop them.
2. **Mix the Butter:**
   - In a medium bowl, combine the softened butter with the grated radishes, chives, parsley, dill (if using), garlic (if using), and lemon juice or vinegar.
   - Mix well until all ingredients are evenly incorporated.
3. **Season:**
   - Season with salt and freshly ground black pepper to taste. Mix again.
4. **Chill:**
   - Transfer the radish and herb butter spread to a serving dish or an airtight container.
   - Refrigerate for at least 30 minutes to allow the flavors to meld.
5. **Serve:**
   - Serve chilled or at room temperature on crusty bread, crackers, or as a flavorful addition to sandwiches.

## Tips:

- **For Extra Flavor:** Add a pinch of smoked paprika or a dash of hot sauce if you like a bit of heat.
- **Make Ahead:** The spread can be made up to a week in advance and stored in the refrigerator.

Enjoy your Radish and Herb Butter Spread—a vibrant, herbaceous, and creamy addition to any meal!

**Minted Pea and Ricotta Salad**

## Ingredients:

- **2 cups fresh or frozen peas** (thawed if frozen)
- **1 cup ricotta cheese**
- **1/4 cup fresh mint leaves**, chopped
- **1/4 cup fresh basil leaves**, chopped (optional)
- **1 tablespoon extra virgin olive oil**
- **1 tablespoon fresh lemon juice**
- **Salt and freshly ground black pepper**, to taste
- **1/4 cup sliced almonds** or **pine nuts** (optional, for added crunch)

## Instructions:

1. **Prepare the Peas:**
   - If using fresh peas, blanch them in boiling water for 2 minutes, then transfer to an ice bath to stop the cooking. Drain well. If using frozen peas, simply thaw and drain.
2. **Make the Salad:**
   - In a large bowl, combine the peas, ricotta cheese, and chopped mint (and basil if using).
   - Drizzle with olive oil and lemon juice. Gently fold the ingredients together until well mixed.
3. **Season:**
   - Season with salt and pepper to taste. Adjust seasoning as needed.
4. **Add Crunch (Optional):**
   - Sprinkle sliced almonds or pine nuts on top for added texture and flavor.
5. **Serve:**
   - Serve immediately or chill in the refrigerator for about 30 minutes to let the flavors meld.

## Tips:

- **For Extra Flavor:** Add a bit of finely grated Parmesan cheese or a sprinkle of red pepper flakes.
- **Make Ahead:** This salad can be prepared a few hours in advance. Just keep it covered in the refrigerator until ready to serve.

Enjoy your Minted Pea and Ricotta Salad—a vibrant, creamy, and refreshing dish perfect for a light lunch or as a side!

**Grilled Peach and Burrata Salad**

## Ingredients:

- **4 ripe peaches**, halved and pitted
- **2 tablespoons olive oil**, plus more for grilling
- **4 oz burrata cheese** (1 ball)
- **4 cups mixed greens** (e.g., arugula, baby spinach, or mixed salad greens)
- **1/4 cup fresh basil leaves**
- **1/4 cup honey** or **balsamic glaze**
- **Salt and freshly ground black pepper**, to taste
- **1/4 cup chopped walnuts** or **toasted almonds** (optional, for added crunch)

## Instructions:

1. **Preheat Grill:**
    - Preheat your grill to medium-high heat.
2. **Grill the Peaches:**
    - Brush the cut sides of the peach halves with olive oil.
    - Place the peaches cut-side down on the grill and cook for 2-3 minutes, or until grill marks appear and the peaches are slightly softened. Flip and cook for an additional 1-2 minutes on the other side. Remove from the grill and let cool slightly.
3. **Prepare the Salad:**
    - In a large bowl, toss the mixed greens with a drizzle of olive oil and a pinch of salt and pepper.
    - Arrange the greens on a serving platter or individual plates.
4. **Assemble the Salad:**
    - Tear the burrata cheese into pieces and scatter over the greens.
    - Slice the grilled peaches into wedges and arrange them on top of the salad.
5. **Finish and Serve:**
    - Drizzle with honey or balsamic glaze.
    - Garnish with fresh basil leaves and chopped walnuts or toasted almonds if using.
    - Season with additional salt and pepper if needed.

## Tips:

- **For Extra Flavor:** Add a sprinkle of sea salt or a few cracks of black pepper over the burrata and peaches.
- **Make Ahead:** Grill the peaches a few hours in advance and store in the refrigerator until ready to assemble the salad.

Enjoy your Grilled Peach and Burrata Salad—a perfect balance of sweet, creamy, and fresh flavors!

**Lemon Thyme Chicken Skewers**

## Ingredients:

- **1 lb (450g) chicken breast or thighs**, cut into bite-sized pieces
- **2 tablespoons olive oil**
- **Zest and juice of 1 lemon**
- **2 tablespoons fresh thyme leaves** (or 1 tablespoon dried thyme)
- **2 cloves garlic**, minced
- **1 teaspoon honey** (optional, for a touch of sweetness)
- **Salt and freshly ground black pepper**, to taste
- **Wooden or metal skewers**

## Instructions:

1. **Prepare the Marinade:**
   - In a bowl, whisk together the olive oil, lemon zest, lemon juice, thyme, garlic, honey (if using), salt, and pepper.
2. **Marinate the Chicken:**
   - Add the chicken pieces to the marinade and toss to coat evenly. Cover and refrigerate for at least 30 minutes, or up to 4 hours for more flavor.
3. **Prepare the Skewers:**
   - If using wooden skewers, soak them in water for 30 minutes to prevent burning. Thread the marinated chicken pieces onto the skewers.
4. **Preheat Grill or Oven:**
   - Preheat your grill to medium-high heat. If using the oven, preheat to 400°F (200°C) and line a baking sheet with foil or parchment paper.
5. **Grill or Bake:**
   - Grill the skewers for 10-12 minutes, turning occasionally, until the chicken is cooked through and has nice grill marks.
   - If baking, place the skewers on the prepared baking sheet and bake for 15-20 minutes, or until the chicken reaches an internal temperature of 165°F (74°C).
6. **Serve:**
   - Serve the chicken skewers hot, garnished with additional lemon wedges or fresh thyme if desired.

## Tips:

- **For Extra Flavor:** Add vegetables like bell peppers, onions, or cherry tomatoes to the skewers.
- **Make Ahead:** Marinate the chicken a day in advance and store it in the refrigerator until ready to cook.

Enjoy your Lemon Thyme Chicken Skewers—zesty, aromatic, and perfect for any outdoor gathering or weeknight meal!

**Zucchini Noodles with Pesto**

## Ingredients:

- **4 medium zucchinis**
- **1 cup basil pesto** (store-bought or homemade)
- **1 tablespoon olive oil** (optional, for sautéing)
- **1/4 cup grated Parmesan cheese** (optional, for garnish)
- **1/4 cup pine nuts** or **toasted almonds** (optional, for garnish)
- **Salt and freshly ground black pepper**, to taste
- **Cherry tomatoes**, halved (optional, for added freshness)

## Homemade Pesto (if making from scratch):

- **2 cups fresh basil leaves**
- **1/4 cup pine nuts** or **walnuts**
- **1/2 cup grated Parmesan cheese**
- **2 cloves garlic**
- **1/2 cup extra virgin olive oil**
- **Salt and freshly ground black pepper**, to taste

## Instructions:

### 1. Prepare the Zucchini Noodles:

- Use a spiralizer, julienne peeler, or mandoline to cut the zucchinis into noodle-like strips. If you don't have these tools, you can slice the zucchini into thin matchsticks.

### 2. Optional: Sauté the Zoodles:

- If you prefer your zucchini noodles a bit softer, heat olive oil in a large skillet over medium heat. Add the zucchini noodles and sauté for 2-3 minutes, or until slightly tender. Season with a pinch of salt and pepper. Drain any excess moisture if needed.

### 3. Toss with Pesto:

- In a large bowl, toss the zucchini noodles with the pesto until well coated.

### 4. Garnish and Serve:

- Transfer the zucchini noodles to serving plates or bowls. Garnish with grated Parmesan cheese, pine nuts or toasted almonds, and halved cherry tomatoes if using.
- Serve immediately.

## Homemade Pesto Instructions:

1. **Combine Ingredients:**
   - In a food processor, combine basil leaves, pine nuts, Parmesan cheese, and garlic.
2. **Blend:**
   - With the processor running, slowly add the olive oil until the pesto reaches your desired consistency. Season with salt and pepper to taste.

## Tips:

- **For Extra Flavor:** Add a squeeze of lemon juice or a sprinkle of red pepper flakes to the pesto.
- **Make Ahead:** You can prepare the pesto in advance and store it in the refrigerator for up to a week.

Enjoy your Zucchini Noodles with Pesto—a light, flavorful, and healthy alternative to traditional pasta dishes!

www.ingramcontent.com/pod-product-compliance
Lightning Source LLC
LaVergne TN
LVHW062048070526
838201LV00080B/2257